CORVETTE

AMERICA'S SPORTS CAR

BY JAY SCHLEIFER

Crestwood House
New York

Maxwell Macmillan Canada
Toronto

Maxwell Macmillan International
New York   Oxford   Singapore   Sydney

To Linda

Crestwood House
Macmillan Publishing Company
866 Third Avenue
New York, NY 10022

Maxwell Macmillan Canada, Inc.
1200 Eglinton Avenue East
Suite 200
Don Mills, Ontario M3C 3N1

Macmillan Publishing Company is part of the Maxwell Communication Group of Companies.

Designed by R Studio T

Printed in the United States of America

10 9 8 7 6 5 4 3 2 1

Library of Congress Cataloging-in-Publication Data

Schleifer, Jay.
Corvette! : America's sports car / Jay Schleifer.
p. cm.—(Cool classics)
Summary: Discusses the history and dynamics of the popular American sports car.
ISBN 0-89686-697-1
1. Corvette automobile—Juvenile literature. [1. Corvette automobile.] I. Title. II. Series.
TL215.C6S36 1992
629.222'2—dc20   91-18096
                                       CIP
                                       AC

CONTENTS

Born in the U.S.A.! Corvettes have always offered style and performance at an affordable price.

◆**1** THIRTY YEARS OF AWESOME

The excitement begins when you first scan the long, low lines. From shark snout to the classic four taillights, the Chevrolet Corvette's looks spell performance. Notice the twin bulges on the hood. Like muscles on a bodybuilder, they promise power inside.

Now swing open the wide door and make yourself at home in the form-fitting bucket seat. Your hands and the controls feel like they were made for each other.

Finally, the moment. Key the big V-8 engine to life and watch as the dashboard lights up like a video game. The red and green numbers and bars that appear look like a cross between Christmas and the Fourth of July. That makes sense. You're about to unwrap a gift of pure fireworks. Now shift into gear and put your foot down on the gas pedal. There's only one word for what happens next:

AWESOME!

For 30 years the formula has been the same: Young person plus Corvette equals excitement. The Vette is more than just a sports car. It's part of what America is all about.

Think about it! Car lovers in other lands may dream of owning a Ferrari or Lamborghini—with their snooty names and blue-blooded histories. But these Italian supercars are millionaire-expensive and hard to come by. They're cars for kings and princes...or people with a royal income.

The Vette—with close to the same performance—is affordable compared to these costly legends. And as for being hard to get, all it takes is a visit to your neighborhood Chevy dealer.

What's more, the Corvette does have a history—a great one. You're about to find out about it.

HARLEY EARL'S DREAM

The time was the 1950s, and the world of American cars was very different than it is now. Instead of the lean, mean, high-tech machines of today, great chrome-toothed dinosaurs roamed the roads. You've probably seen pictures of them: chunky lumps of metal with rocketship tailfins that grew higher each year. With monster engines some of these cars were fast off the line. But they bucked and swayed like woozy camels at the first curve. And they stopped just about as surely.

Deep in America's car factories, **designers** and **engineers** built these rolling palaces by the millions. That's what it seemed the public wanted. But many designers dreamed of building a different kind of car: the "sports car."

Sports cars—like the Jaguar, MG and Porsche—ruled the roads in Europe. They were smaller than U.S. cars, and less powerful. But on a curvy road a sports car could run rings around the American models.

U.S. designers felt America should have sports machines too. But few had the power within their own companies to bring such dreams to life.

One who did have such power was Harley Earl, top designer at giant General Motors. Earl loved the sports cars of Europe and felt GM should build one. His bosses, of course, disagreed. They refused to spend the millions the project would cost. Luckily, Earl had just the tool to convince them.

Each year GM put together a car show called Motorama. The show traveled from city to city and was used to introduce GM's new models to the public.

Harley Earl

To lure buyers into coming, GM created special models called "dream cars." These machines were totally unlike the models on sale. Dream cars featured wild ideas and supermodern looks. Some were more like aircraft than cars. The public loved them!

Earl had a plan for the 1953 Motorama. If he could design a hot two-seat sports car, his bosses might let him show it as a dream

> **You could get Harley Earl's original Corvette in any color you wanted . . . as long as it was "polo white"!**

machine. Then maybe, if buyers liked it, GM would allow the new model to be sold.

The problem was that the Motorama was just a few months away. Earl would have to work fast.

In the weeks that followed, Earl and his designers shaped the new sportster day and night, seven days a week.

For ideas Earl turned to the sports cars he'd seen in Europe. He gave the new machine clean, low lines that seemed a cross between a Jaguar and a Ferrari. Then he added touches like sporty wheels and wire-mesh stone guards over the headlights.

Unlike most models of the day, there wasn't a tailfin in sight on the dream car. But Earl's designers couldn't resist adding tiny rocketship taillights to an otherwise clean body shape. This was an *American* sports car, after all.

Earl next turned his design into a full-size model. It had no running parts, but otherwise it seemed just like a real car. Then he called in his bosses for a look.

Earl needn't have worried about their reactions. When the top man at GM's Chevrolet Division saw the model, he actually jumped up and down in excitement, right in his business suit! The car won a place in the Motorama exhibit. What's more, the Chevy boss said that if the public liked it, he'd put it up for sale as a Chevrolet. Now it was Earl's turn to jump for joy!

The car looked great. But looks were only the start. Now the nonworking *model* had to be turned into a real, running *car*.

Working from the bottom up, engineers started with a low-slung frame like the ones European machines rode on. They shoved the engine forward and the seats back for a solid stance. Then they stiffened up the springs and shocks so the car would lean less on turns.

There was no time to come up with a new high-performance

engine, so the standard Chevy Blue Flame Six was popped in. This ancient power plant had begun life as a truck engine, and it was used in every plain-Jane Chevy on the road. But the engineers made some changes and raised the horsepower from less than 100 to 150.

While most European sportsters had a stick shift, engineers gave the new American sports car an automatic. GM felt that's what U.S. buyers wanted. In other ways, though, the car was very European. Instead of power windows, plastic sheets were mounted on top of the doors. The same system was used in MGs and other roadsters. When not needed, these side curtains were taken off and tossed into the trunk.

With the Motorama show now closer than ever, Earl lacked the time to build the usual steel body. Instead he shaped it from a new "miracle plastic" called **fiberglass.** Fiberglass was easy to work with and would never rust, but it had its own problems. One was that it didn't carry electricity the way a metal body did. That meant the body could not act as part of the car's electrical system, as a steel body did.

Engineers found this out when they finished wiring the car and then discovered that nothing worked! No lights! No radio! Not even the horn worked! Extra wiring had to be added at the last minute.

Now the car was almost ready for the show. But one vital item was missing—a name. In the planning stages, the car had been called Project Opel, and EX-122. But something classier was needed.

Chevy liked names that began with a c (Camaro, Caprice, Chevelle), so that's where the search began. It ended when the car reminded someone of a kind of fast British warship. The ship was called—you guessed it—a **corvette**. Finally, the first and only Chevrolet Corvette rolled out to meet the world.

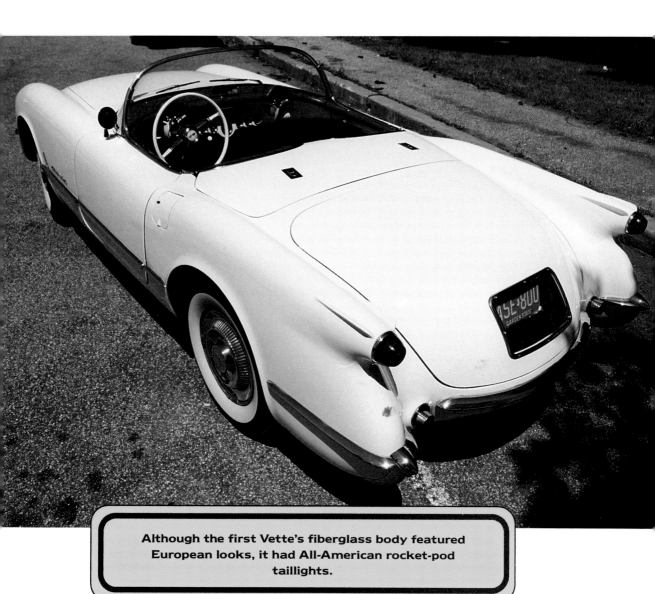

Although the first Vette's fiberglass body featured
European looks, it had All-American rocket-pod
taillights.

For the Motorama the car was finished in gleaming white and
fitted with hot-red leather seats. As it slowly turned under the
spotlights, more than eight million showgoers saw it. They loved it.
"Where can we get one?" car lovers asked in city after city. "How
much?...And how soon?"

GM knew that there was only one way to handle the fuss: Put the
car into production.

3 THE DREAM ALMOST DIES

Chevrolet had a hit! But it also had a problem. To build the new Corvette, a factory had to be created at a cost of millions of dollars. The risks were gigantic.

Even worse, nobody at GM had ever sold a real sports car. Who would the buyers be? Chevrolet wondered. Certainly not Motorama visitors. They might want the car. But if asked to put up thousands of dollars to buy one, most showgoers would melt right back into the crowd.

Chevrolet made what seemed the right move at the time. The company went after America's rich and famous—high-fashion folks who just *had* to have the latest in anything. Surely they'd love the car...and they'd have the money to buy it.

There was only one word for what followed: *disaster*! As planned, almost everyone loved the Vette's looks. But those who'd driven European sports cars saw the car as a weak copy of the real thing. They hated the wimpy Blue Flame Six engine and the automatic gearbox. " 'Real' drivers shift for themselves," they said.

At the same time the fashion crowd turned up their noses at the Vette. Where were the little extras a real-life dream machine should have...like power windows that raised and lowered at the touch of a button? In fact, *where were the windows?* Surely not those plastic things! "Chevrolet," they seemed to say, "you have *got* to be kidding!"

Chevy hoped to sell 20,000 Corvettes each year. But the first year only 300 rolled out onto the roads. That was about as many cars as the company usually built in an hour!

Things normally start slowly when a new car is built for the first time. Workers have to learn their jobs and get the bugs out of the machinery. But the next year, 1954, only about 3,600 Corvettes were sold.

In 1955 most car models enjoyed fantastic sales. Not the Corvette. Sales dropped to fewer than 700. Many Chevy dealers no longer wanted this pretty but slow-selling model taking up space in their showrooms.

GM bosses shook their heads. They wanted to forget about the Corvette and cut their losses. Harley Earl's dream had turned into a nightmare.

 ## 4 "BEAT FORD!"

By all rights there should have been no 1956 Corvette. In fact, the '56 was one of the best Vettes ever. What saved the car?

Surprisingly, one answer is *Ford.*

In those years, even more than now, Ford was Chevy's great rival. The opposing companies fought it out year after year, trying to sell more cars than anyone else in the world.

Like gunfighters on a western street, Chevy and Ford watched each other's every move. Some time in the early 1950s, Ford designers became aware of the Corvette. They quickly got to work on their own two-seater. And in 1955, with the Corvette nearly dead on its feet, they put their Vette beater on sale. The new Ford Thunderbird had flown into town.

The T-Bird, as many called it, was everything the Corvette was not. It was powered by a V-8 engine, as opposed to the Vette's six. It offered buyers a choice of automatic or stick shift. The car could be had with power steering and power brakes. And, best of all, the

Ford introduced the Thunderbird in 1954, and the Vette suddenly had competition.

Bird had real windows, power-operated at that!

From the day it appeared, the Thunderbird was a sales smash! For every Corvette sold Ford sold *16* T-Birds. It was almost too much for Chevrolet to bear. Suddenly GM bosses didn't seem to care how much money they lost on the Vette. *Spend whatever you need to improve the car,* GM told Chevrolet, *but beat Ford!* The result was the fantastic '56.

Suddenly Vette had it all—beginning with a new engine. As soon as it was able, Chevy snuffed out the Vette's Blue Flame Six. The company had just come out with a hot V-8 for its sedans. Now this dream of an engine was fitted into the Corvette. With this one change, horsepower skyrocketed from a measly 150 to an explosive 226. It was as if someone had stuffed a second engine under the hood.

And engine weight actually dropped. Chevy had found a way to make an eight-cylinder engine that weighed less than a six! Lighter but with much more power, the new motor was a real roadburner! And it was so well designed that the same basic motor—enlarged, updated and computer controlled—still powers the Vette today!

Buyers finally had their choice of gearboxes—stick or automatic. And Harley Earl and his designers outdid themselves on the body. If the first Vette was good-looking, this one was gorgeous.

Gone were the rocket taillights and sunken headlights. Instead, the new look lunged forward, as if to say "Get out of my way!" An aggressive bulge appeared above and behind the front wheels, as if the tires were throwing up dust just standing still. And new, two-tone colors made the new shape even more exciting. Even now, few cars can turn heads like a red-and-white '56 Vette.

The seating area was improved too. And—finally learning its lesson—Chevy gave the car real windows!

In 1957 Chevy improved the car even more. A new system called ramjet **fuel injection** could be added to the engine at extra cost. First developed for high-powered aircraft, fuel injection forced gas into the engine instead of just letting it drift in through a carburetor. That kicked engine output to a blazing 283 horsepower. Few cars could beat a "fuelie" Vette when the light turned green.

The '56 second generation Vette was improved inside and out.
(Inset) In 1957 buyers could add fuel injection to the engine.

The Vette was now fast, fun and full of fire. But with the T-Bird way ahead in sales, Chevy needed a way to show buyers that the Vette had changed. They found one: Race the Corvette.

Suddenly Corvettes began showing up on race courses all over the nation. For the first time an American car ran wheel to wheel with the great sports machines of Europe. Vettes ran against Jaguars, Porsches, even Ferraris, with a real chance to win.

5 THE MARK OF ZORA

In making the Corvette a true performance car, Chevrolet had the use of a secret weapon. No, not the new V-8 engine or the fuel-injection system. Their weapon was one of the most talented auto engineers of all time: Zora Arkus-Duntov.

As you might expect from his tongue-twisting name, Duntov was a European, the son of Russian immigrants. He had worked for an English carmaker, but he felt there might be better jobs in America. So he wrote to GM to inquire about working for them.

Duntov was hired, but not to work on Corvettes. In fact, his first job on the Vette was minor: to find out why exhaust gas was dirtying the rear bodywork. But, as he later told a writer for a car magazine, "I borrowed one and thought it was the most beautiful car I had ever seen, even though the engine was a letdown and the handling not good. I took it on myself to give the car better handling. This was not part of my regular job...just fiddling on the side."

As part of this "fiddling," Zora built a special Vette that could reach a speed of more than 150 mph. This impressed his bosses. Soon more work on the Vette began to come Duntov's way. In time he was made chief engineer in charge of Corvette.

This quiet, white-haired genius worked on Corvettes until the day he retired. In fact, all Vettes built between 1954 and 1974 bear "the Mark of Zora." It's for good reason that Zora Arkus-Duntov earned the nickname "Mr. Corvette."

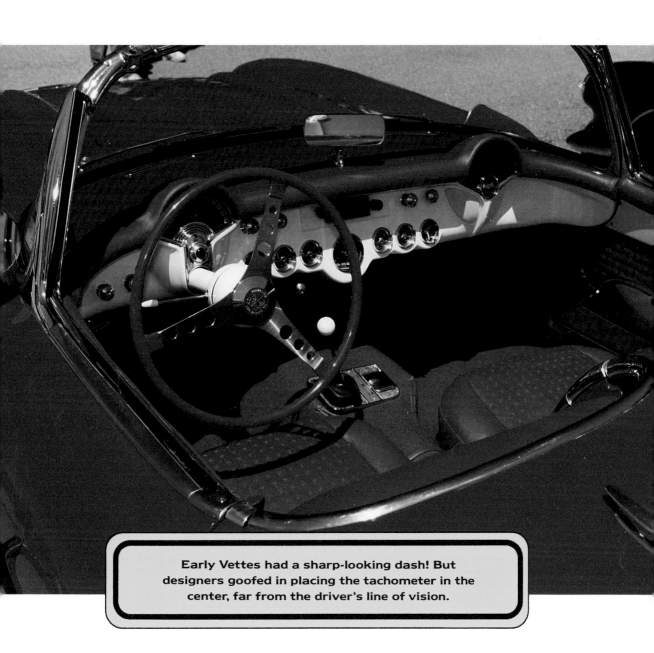

Early Vettes had a sharp-looking dash! But designers goofed in placing the tachometer in the center, far from the driver's line of vision.

6 THE NEVER-NEVER CORVETTE

Every sport has its top events. Baseball has the All-Star game and the World Series. And no football game tops the Super Bowl. In the same way sports-car fans of the 1950s had their top races—held each year at Sebring, Florida, and Le Mans, France.

Though Corvettes were winning at local tracks across America, Chevy knew that the Vette had to compete—and win—at these top races if it was ever to be taken seriously.

Duntov told them, though, that as good as the street Vette had become, it was not good enough for Sebring or Le Mans. Ferrari, Porsche, and Jaguar built special cars for these races: all-out track machines that no street sports car could match. If Chevy wanted to win they'd have to do the same.

So it was that a mysterious trailer truck arrived one day at Sebring. When the doors to the trailer opened, out rolled one of the most beautiful racing cars of all time. It looked something like a Corvette, especially around the front. But otherwise the car was totally different.

There was one thing every fan recognized, however. The car was painted a shiny blue and white: the racing colors of the United States. The car was the incredible Corvette SS.

Like the original Corvette, this first all-out Corvette racer had been built in just a few short months. Duntov and his crew had had the money and talents of GM to work with—something smaller builders like Ferrari could only dream of. But Duntov knew that, big as it was, the giant American company had never competed seriously in sports-car racing. He also knew that on the racetrack experience could be even more important than money.

As a shortcut to the winner's circle, Duntov had borrowed important ideas from the Europeans. The SS body shape was much like that of the D-Type Jaguar, a race winner of the time. Its frame design was copied, in part, from a Mercedes-Benz racer. Like the Mercedes, it was made of lightweight metal tubing instead of heavy beams.

The engine, however, was born in the United States. It was a lightweight version of the regular Vette's "fuelie" V-8. But Chevy had kicked the horsepower to 307 from the standard 283.

Most important, the usual fiberglass body was replaced with **magnesium**. This magic metal was expensive, but it was also incredibly light. The completed car rolled out at just 1,850 pounds, a half a ton less than a street Vette.

As additional insurance, Duntov borrowed something else from the European teams: their best drivers. World champion Juan Manuel Fangio, perhaps the greatest wheelman ever to race, agreed to pilot the Corvette SS at Sebring. His teammate was Stirling Moss of England, the number-two driver in the world.

The plan was to build two cars. One was a half-finished model, called a "mule," for testing. The other was the car for the actual race.

Things looked great when Fangio put the mule through its first tests at Sebring. He had no trouble breaking his own lap record, set in a Ferrari the year before.

But then the problems began. Though Duntov's people rushed like demons to complete the actual race car, it arrived later than planned. Fangio and Moss got tired of waiting and signed to drive Italian Maseratis instead. Other drivers signed on, but nobody could really replace the world's two best.

Next, cooling and braking problems were discovered. And when the finished SS finally did start, a small part broke after just **21**

23 laps, putting the car out for the day. None of the car's problems were major. And the SS had shown great stuff when it was running. Duntov looked forward to putting a four-car team on the starting line at Le Mans a few months later.

The car was soon out of racing for good, however. As 1950s cars had become more powerful, highway deaths were rising. Safety groups began putting pressure on car companies to stop talking about how fast their cars were and to sell them in some other way.

In 1961 the trunk lid flattened out and the famous four taillights appeared for the first time.

The companies agreed to do this—and to ban any activity that had to do with racing or speed.

The finished SS and its mule model were returned to GM, with an order never to race again. The order was obeyed for the finished SS, which has since lived quietly in a GM museum. But the mule—which Fangio had driven to a new record—had a different fate. It sat under a sheet in a GM garage for nearly three years, apparently forgotten. Then one day it quietly vanished.

Who took it and why? That's a story you're about to read.

 **FISH OUT OF WATER**

Though beautiful and fast, the '56 and '57 Corvettes still were not sales successes. The '57 sold less than 7,000 cars, far short of the 20,000 GM had wanted. Only a few hundred of the advanced fuel-injected models left the factory.

Ford's Thunderbird was no longer a threat. Ford had made the car a four-seater. So the two machines no longer even played in the same league. Without this competition, it began to look as though the Vette would never really take off.

A kind of sleepiness now seemed to set in at Corvette. The car got bigger, heavier, and less graceful. It grew four headlights and all kinds of chrome doodads. Sales increased, but it seemed as though the designers and engineers were no longer as interested in their pride and joy.

In fact, nothing was further from the truth. Harley Earl had retired, but Duntov and the new GM chief designer, William L. Mitchell, were hard at work developing a totally new kind of Corvette.

"Bill" Mitchell had joined GM in the 1930s. He'd been Harley Earl's number-two man for years. Earl liked performance cars, but Mitchell was crazy about them. And for years, he'd dreamed of racing a car of his own design.

In the Corvette SS mule lying corpselike under a sheet, Mitchell saw his chance. He began to pester his bosses to let him have the car and race it.

At first the answer was no. Top GM people were to stay away from racing, period.

Mitchell was stubborn. "I got my start in racing," he wrote to his bosses. "It's in my blood."

In time Mitchell was told he could have the SS, with two conditions: First, he had to pay for it with his own money, and second, he had to change it so that no one could recognize the car as coming from GM. Another reason he got it may have been that he was driving his bosses crazy!

Mitchell quickly had the car moved to a secret room at GM called "Studio X." There Duntov and a small group of lucky designers, often working after hours, rebuilt it.

First, they fixed the problems that had come up at Sebring. Then a new body was designed: flat on top, curved on the bottom, and painted fire-engine red.

Finally the car got a new name. Mitchell was a sports fisherman, and the new shape reminded him of one of the creatures he hunted in the oceans. He named the car after that creature: the Sting Ray.

Driven by Dr. Dick Thompson, "the Flying Dentist," the Sting Ray was a top finisher at many races in the early 1960s.

In time GM watchers caught on to what Mitchell and his friends were up to. They realized that the car was a GM project. (The fact that Mitchell and Duntov were always hanging around the mystery

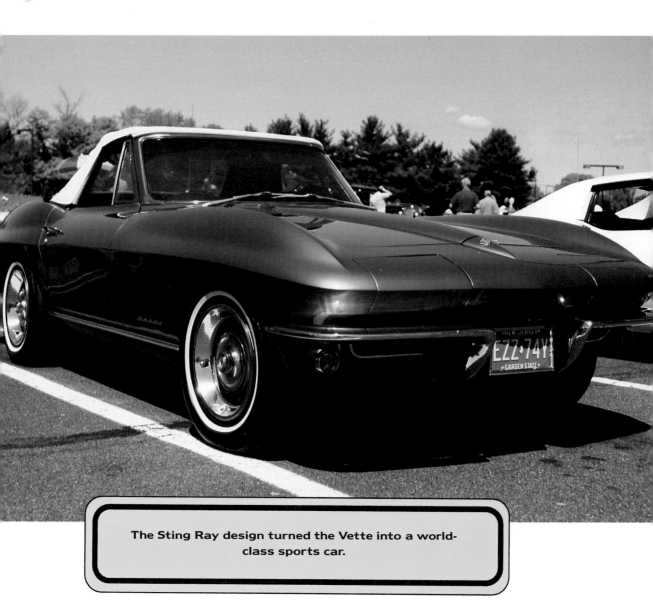

The Sting Ray design turned the Vette into a world-class sports car.

machine didn't help!) Finally Mitchell got the word from the top: park it for good. He resold the car to GM.

Repainted silver, and with Corvette nametags, the Sting Ray took its place next to the original SS. GM now considers it a proud part of Corvette history—though at the time company executives wanted nothing to do with it!

⬡ 8 THE NEW CORVETTE

By 1962 Corvette had reached the point where it had to change or die. The 1956 design, much of which dated back to 1953, was getting really old.

What's more, there were hot new European sports machines on the market. Jaguar had built the bullet-shaped and bullet-fast E-Type. And Porsche had brought out the 911, the first all-new model in the company's history.

There were also rumors that Chevy's old rival, Ford, was up to something.

Fortunately Chevy was up to something, too. For years Duntov had been working on making the Corvette better. But he felt he'd done all he could with the old design. He wanted a totally new Corvette.

The change he wanted most was at the rear. The first Vette had what's called a **solid rear axle**. This design goes back to horse-and-buggy days. Both rear wheels are on the ends of a massive steel beam. When one side hits a bump, the other side rises too. The rear of the car can actually hop off the ground, causing poor handling and a jarring ride.

Duntov knew that there was a better system, called **i.r.s.** (independent rear suspension). An i.r.s. car has its back wheels mounted separately. When one hits a bump, the other is not affected. The car handles better, and the ride is smoother. The new Jaguar had i.r.s., as did the Porsche. Duntov wanted it on the Corvette.

The problem: To keep costs down, the Vette used parts right off Chevy's big sedans. None had i.r.s. Special parts would therefore be needed. And too few Corvettes were sold to pay the cost of the new system.

Still Duntov insisted on it.

Bill Mitchell was also revving like a racer to do a new Vette. He knew just what it should look like—his Sting Ray special! What's more, he wanted to try a new body style: a closed-top model called a coupe, to be sold alongside the usual open roadster. And most everyone on the project wanted the new Vette to be smaller, lighter and better balanced than the old one.

Top GM bosses fought these changes until Duntov promised that his hot new Vette would sell not the 20,000 they wanted—but 30,000! Now he was talking GM's language! His bosses finally agreed to build the car.

The new car, named the Corvette Sting Ray, went on sale as a 1963 model. Sports-car lovers took a look, took a ride and cheered! It was the best Vette ever. For the first time, said magazine writers, America had a true world-class sports car. Only the engine and gearbox were leftovers from the past, and they'd always been among the best parts. Everything else was totally new—and top of the line.

One Sting Ray feature nearly caused a war inside GM. Mitchell had decided that his bullet-top coupe should have a thick bar down the center of the rear window. He felt it made the car look sleeker.

Duntov said no; all the bar did was make it hard to see what was behind you. He wanted it off.

Mitchell fought back. "Take that off," he told GM bosses, "and you might as well forget the whole thing!"

They argued back and forth. Neither would give up. Finally top GM executives made the decision for both of them. The bar would be on the car for 1963 only, then it was history.

The car that resulted is called the split-window coupe. It's one of the rarest and most valuable old Vettes.

Designer Bill Mitchell insisted on the split rear window. GM executives let him have it for one year—1963.

Over the next four years, GM continued to improve the Sting Ray. The car became cleaner and sharper. A new **disk-brake** system replaced the old drums for better stopping power, and other changes were made to improve the handling.

Thousands of Corvettes have been built since the Sting Ray passed into history in 1967. But many people still think of it as the finest Corvette of them all.

Ford had fattened the Thunderbird to four seats, but that didn't end Ford's threat to the Corvette.

In fact, Ford was about to begin the greatest sports-car program in American auto history. One part of the program resulted in the famous Mustang. But another was more of a danger to the Vette. Ford had gotten together with a racing driver, Caroll Shelby, to build a vicious machine called the Cobra.

Making a Cobra was simple. Shelby pulled the little four-cylinder engine out of a lightweight English sports car called the AC Ace. He replaced it with a Ford V-8. In doing so, he added

The Cobra was a lightweight English body with a Ford V-8 engine. It was loud and fast, and ate Corvettes for lunch!

blinding speed to already good handling. Cobras began eating privately raced Sting Rays for lunch at racetracks all over America. Ford engineers could barely stop giggling.

To Chevy, *Cobra* was a fighting word. And Duntov quickly began to craft a weapon to fight back: the legendary Corvette Grand Sport.

Duntov began with the basic Sting Ray coupe. First stop was the engine room, where the car's basic 327-cubic-inch V-8 was enlarged to 377 cubes.

Where the normal V-8 put out about 350 horses, the GS version pumped 550. The engine had to turn an amazing 6,400 times a minute to do it, nearly twice normal speed. One race fan compared the sound of all this—produced as it was with no mufflers—to the noise of a World War II bombing raid.

To handle the power, the GS got heavy-duty parts all over. Fat steel tubes ran around the seats and over the top for crash protection. Then the car was put on a crash diet, with holes drilled through anything not needed for strength.

Final weight was a feathery 2,000 pounds—almost half a ton less than a street Vette. With so much power and so little weight, performance was earth-shaking!

Although the GS was an out-and-out racing car, Chevy still tossed in a few luxuries. The car had wall-to-wall carpeting and even a shiny chrome gearshift knob.

By this time, GM had relaxed its racing ban, so the car could take on the Cobras. But to make the GS legal under racing rules, Chevy had to build 125 copies. Five were quickly bolted together and sent out to do battle. Race officials got a promise that the rest were on the way.

First race results were promising. A GS won its class the first time out, beating two Cobras and even a Ferrari.

But then history repeated itself! Once again, GM became nervous about racing, and another ban came down from above. The short life of the GS as a racing champion came to an end.

But history repeated itself in another way. Just as the SS rose again when Bill Mitchell raced it privately as the Sting Ray, three GS racers were secretly sold to private owners, who continued racing them. They never totally stopped Cobra, which continued to enjoy factory help from Ford. But they made life difficult for the snakes. And that gave Chevy engineers something to giggle about for a change!

 **SHARK ATTACK!**

In the 1960s car builders tried to change the looks of their machines every few years. The companies felt that this kept up buyer interest and sales. So almost as soon as the '63 Sting Ray went on sale, Chevy began working on a new Corvette to go on sale in 1968.

Bill Mitchell's designers knew that their boss loved big-game fish, and that gave them an idea. If the first Mitchell Vette was a Sting Ray, the new one would look like an even more exciting sea creature—the shark.

You can see it even in the first drawings. They show a low, pointed nose and a curved body ending in an upswept tail. Some models were even painted with light-colored bottoms that turned darker toward the top, just like the great white in the movie *Jaws.* All that was missing was a fin to cut through the water and scare swimmers!

GM had spent a ton of money for the i.r.s. rear end and other special parts on the Sting Ray. So they decided to leave the **31**

In 1968 the Vette was redesigned to look like Chevy's "shark" show cars. This design lasted for 15 years!

Corvette pretty much unchanged under the skin. Only the look would be totally new.

One engineering change was made, though. The new body allowed for a massive engine—much bigger than the small-block V-8s usually used in the Vette. That was because the 1960s had become the age of the **musclecar**.

This had started when, almost as a joke, Pontiac stuffed a huge V-8 from their biggest sedan into one of their smallest cars—just to see what would happen.

What happened was that they created a new kind of car called the GTO. It delivered incredible performance at a cheap price.

Young buyers quickly turned the GTO into a major hit. And now every company was shoehorning gigantic engines into small bodies.

As America's performance car, the Corvette had to follow along. Engines as big as 454 cubic inches were jammed into the Vette body.

The result was unbalanced and nose heavy. But it could pin your shoulders to the seat and blur your eyesight, even if it had trouble making a proper turn. The height of the action came with a big-engine Vette called the L88. This monster pumped out 585 horsepower—more than the racetrack GS!

The L88 was expensive, though, and the insurance was often more so. Only a few hundred were built. That's probably lucky. Highways might have caved in had there been more!

To get i.r.s., Duntov had promised 30,000 sales in a year. By 1970 sales were pushing 40,000! But something important had changed. The Corvette was no longer a finely balanced sports car, designed to run wheel to wheel with Porsche or Ferrari. It had become, some car magazines said, a "hot rod, plastic flash." *Road & Track* called it "The Animal."

To many buyers, that was as it should be. And the shark design was often customized for even more stunning looks.

The Animal lived for a long time. The shark design was first built in 1968, with a new Corvette planned for the early 1970s. But suddenly Chevy engineers had a lot more to do than design new Corvettes.

America had realized it had major problems with the automobile. There were gas shortages, and fuel prices shot out of sight. The air over large cities was thick with smoke from auto tailpipes. And deaths on the highway had passed 50,000 a year—about as many Americans as died in the entire Vietnam War.

The government now passed strict laws on fuel economy, pollution and safety. Automakers had to build new parts into their cars by law. The Vette would just have to limp along year after year with small changes while engineers tackled these more important problems.

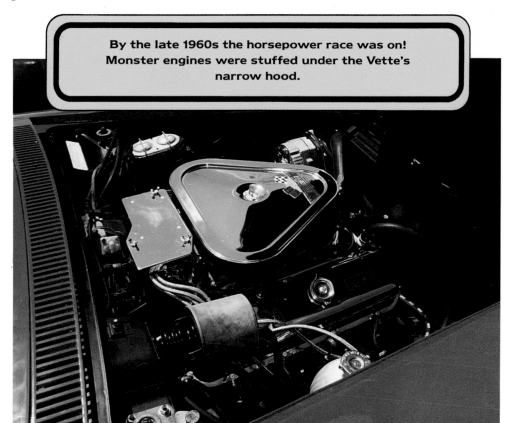

By the late 1960s the horsepower race was on! Monster engines were stuffed under the Vette's narrow hood.

The shark design, oddly still called Sting Ray—started out as a four-year design. It ended up a *15-year* design. The auto world would not see a really new Corvette again until model year 1984!

The shark design featured a T-top roof.

11 MIDENGINE MADNESS

Fifteen years is a long time between new Vettes. But there were always hints of what the next Corvette might be like. One story that went on and on in those years was that the new car would carry its engine in the middle of the car.

European engineers had begun this trend. They'd found that a sports car could have better balance if the heavy engine was placed smack-dab in the center. Many racers had begun to use this location. So did Ferrari and other supercars built for the street.

Chevy fed the rumor by building one midengine "dream Corvette" after another. These cars were shown at auto shows, just as the first Vette had been. With little to report about the regular Vette, car magazines kept the rumors hot. "Any time we had to sell more copies," said one editor, "we'd get an artist to draw a hot-looking midengine sports car. Then we'd run the drawing on the cover with the headline 'Is this the New Corvette?' It always worked!"

Deep within Chevrolet, engineers were thinking of doing a mid-engine machine. Duntov favored it. So did Bill Mitchell. But no other GM car was mid-engined, so many special parts would need to be made that could only be used on the Vette. The bill was too high even for GM to swallow.

Then in the early 1970s GM began to think of making an even bigger change to their cars. The company played around with a new kind of engine called the **Wankel rotary**.

The Wankel tossed away all the usual pistons, valves and many other parts. Instead, power came from a triangle-shaped piston that spun in circles at incredible speed. A tiny Wankel as small and light as a four had as much power as a big V-8. And it was so compact you could put it almost anywhere in the car. GM at one time planned to put Wankels in many of its cars. (In fact, the Wankel design did finally power a two-seater—Mazda's RX-7.)

Mitchell's designers created a fabulous new midengine Corvette to carry the Wankel. They called the car the Aerovette for its ability to slice through the wind. The Wankel quickly began having problems at GM, however. It burned too much gas and created too much pollution, and so it was dropped. But Mitchell refused to junk the Aerovette. With Duntov's help, he fitted a standard V-8 into the body and continued to push for the car to be produced as the new Corvette.

At one time the car was close to being the 1980 Corvette. But by now the power of the designers was not as great as in the days when Mitchell demanded and got a bar down the center of the rear window. The head of GM finally took Mitchell aside and told him that as long as the shark design kept selling, there was no need for a new Vette.

GM asks all its top people to retire at age 65. Mitchell reached that age in 1978. "They took the most beautiful car ever styled and let it hang around," he said when he left GM. "And now without me to sit on 'em, it's not going anywhere."

After leaving GM he worked on new designs on his own for a while and collected cars he liked. He died in 1989, a split-window Sting Ray in his garage.

 **TODAY'S CORVETTE**

By 1980 the car world had changed again. Many of the auto's problems were being solved. It might—just might—be time for some exciting cars again, designers thought.

The Corvette team was new as well. Bill Mitchell had retired. Zora Arkus-Duntov had also reached age 65. After nearly 20 years as "Mr. Corvette," his time at the wheel was over.

A new Corvette designer, Jerry Palmer, took over. (Palmer would also be the mastermind behind the slick and very European-looking Chevy Camaro that would appear in 1982.) He and his

artists were itching to try a lean new look for America's sports car.

Replacing Duntov as chief engineer was David McLellan. Dave was no "seat of the pants" car builder. His tools were computers, not wrenches. Anyone who knew these men knew that the next Vette would be high-tech all the way. In their hands the old "animal" design was a dead duck!

Their first decision was that the new car would be the best that GM could build. There would be no argument over using the right parts, as there was over the i.r.s. rear end. The new Vette would be a showcase of what the world's biggest car company could do when it really wanted to. If the car cost more than before, that's the way it would be.

McLellan decided that the front-engine design was still the way to go. Midengine designs took up too much space, and he wanted a comfortable car. Next he created a whole new **chassis.** It looked like it came right off a Lotus or a Ferrari. And in fact, many of the ideas for the '84 Corvette came from the world's finest cars.

Meanwhile, Jerry Palmer put some of the old Vette into the new Vette. He even kept the four round taillights used since 1961. But the new car was much smoother and cleaner.

The designers paid attention to everything—even under the hood. They covered the engine with a sleek air cleaner and they even chose the colors of the electrical wires. Then they made the hood open like a clamshell, partly to better show off their work.

Inside, dials gave way to a digital light show on the dash. Green, yellow, and red numbers and bar graphs lit up as soon as the key was turned. Some felt the new dash was gimmicky and hard to read, but others loved the "Star Wars" look.

When the new Vette was introduced, Chevy called it a 1984 model. The last old-style Vette had been a 1982 model. Strangely there is no 1983 car, even though that year would have marked the Corvette's 30th birthday.

Vette owners have always customized their cars. This is a '74 with aero body parts and an awesome stripe job!

**By 1982 the shark design was ready for replacement.
This pretty coupe was one of the last of the breed.**

As you might expect, sales of the first new Vette in 15 years took off like a rocket. The car was a hit even though it cost more than ever before—some $20,000.

In 1986 a convertible model was added—at a price tag over $30,000. Still, the car was cheap compared to Europe's best. A Porsche might cost twice as much. And you could buy a three-bedroom house for less than a Ferrari!

How long will the "new" Corvette last? Magazines reported the car would remain pretty much unchanged for at least ten years, and maybe beyond that.

13 ALL HAIL THE "KING OF THE HILL"

Work on the current Corvette was complete by 1983. But the Corvette's builders soon found another project to get excited about. They'd decided to build the "King of the Hill" Corvette.

The project started with a question: Could America build a car that could compete with *anything* Europe could throw against it—including the so-called supercars from Ferrari or Lamborghini?

In a way it was the same question that had led to the first Vette: Could America take on the world?

Dave McLellan knew that a big part of that answer lay in the Corvette's engine room. The regular Vette used Chevy's standard small-block V-8. It was a solid engine, but low-tech. For example, it used just two valves to move gas in and out of each cylinder. Those valves were opened by a system of long pushrods running through the engine. The basic design could be traced to the days of the Model-T Ford.

McLellan knew a better way. Put *four* valves into each cylinder, to let more fuel in and more exhaust out. An engine that "breathes" better has more power. He also installed a more compact **overhead-camshaft system** to work the valves instead of the old pushrod setup.

Thus was born the four-overhead-cam 32-valve LT-5 engine. This high-tech roadburner is the same size as Corvette's regular engine, but it has nearly twice the power! The car that carries it looks much like the regular Vette, except for a tiny badge on the tail. The badge reads "ZR-1." It might as well read "high explosives"!

Try zero to 60 in less time than it takes to read this sentence—

**Welcome to horsepower city, U.S.A. The engine in the
ZR-1 features four cams, 32 valves and a top speed
pushing 190 miles an hour!**

under five seconds. Try a punch that feels like an F-15 jet on afterburners, with cornering to match. Try a top speed that's closer to *200 mph* than 100. When the ZR-1 began hitting the highway, Ferraris everywhere began to seek shelter.

The Corvette ZR-1 is so speed-shattering that Chevy includes a special key to lock out half the power. Owners use it to keep parking-lot attendants from getting into trouble. Sorry, guys. You'll just have to collect a few more tips and buy your own ZR-1. It will take quite a few tips. At last look, the price tag on this heaviest Chevy read somewhere north of $60,000.

14 IS THIS THE NEXT CORVETTE?

America's sports car, the Chevrolet Corvette, was born in 1953. In its early years, it was a slow seller that almost died before its third birthday. Now, nearly 40 years later, the Corvette is one of America's great auto-success stories—a world-class winner that does America proud wherever it goes. More than a million Vettes have rolled forward to do battle with Europe's—and now Japan's—best on road and track.

What will this Cool Classic's future be? Only GM knows—and they're not telling. But there are some interesting hints. You see one of them here. It's the fabulous Corvette Indy.

The "New Corvette" was a classic when introduced in 1984. It featured a high-tech engine and chassis.

First shown in 1985 the Indy is like no Vette ever. The Corvette has always been basically square—low and sleek, but square. The Indy features a whole new look, somewhere between prowling wildcat and Star Wars. There isn't a straight line on it.

What's under the skin is just as much of a breakthrough. The midengine layout is back, but that's just for openers. The rest of the story is told in fours.

- Four-wheel drive puts the power to work on all corners of the car.
- Four-wheel antilock disk brakes make for controlled and fade-free stops in any weather.
- Four-wheel *steering*—yes, you read that right—make moves clean and sharp.
- And at all four corners is a magic invention called four-wheel active suspension.

Developed by Lotus of England (the famous racecar builder is now owned by GM), **active suspension** is the first totally new spring system in years. Instead of taking on bumps as they come, active "reads" the road electronically. When a hole or bump is in range, computer-controlled pumps ram the wheels up or down for the best control position before they hit the bump. Ride and handling have never been this good before.

Active suspension also lets a car take turns without the usual body lean. The car can even be made to lean *into* a turn like a motorcycle, rather than leaning away as cars have always done. With so much control, cornering speeds can be higher than ever.

All these goodies cost a king's ransom now. And no one knows how many will ever show up on a Vette you can buy. But one thing is certain: About the time you're ready to buy one, the Cool Classic called Corvette will be alive...well...and more exciting than ever.

GLOSSARY/INDEX

active suspension 46 A computer-controlled system that actively pumps a car's wheels up or down to balance the effect on the car of bumps or holes in the road.

chassis 39 The underparts of a car.

corvette 10 A small, fast warship. Chevrolet's sports car was named after this type of vessel.

designer 6 Creator of a car's appearance and general layout.

disk brakes 28 A stopping system that works by pressing on a spinning disk connected to the wheel. Disk brakes are especially good for stopping in wet weather.

engineer 6 Person who decides how the car's engine and other parts and systems will work.

fiberglass 10, 21 A plasticlike material used in the body of the Corvette. Fiberglass is easy to work with and does not rust. Also used in skis, crash helmets, and other items.

fuel injection 15, 23 A system that actively pumps the fuel-air mixture into an engine rather than having it drift in. Replaces the carburetor.

i.r.s. (independent rear suspension) 26, 31, 39 Way of mounting rear wheels separately so that when one hits a bump, the other is not affected.

magnesium 21 An extremely light but strong metal.

musclecar 34 Small car with a very large engine. Popular in the 1960s. The first musclecar was the 1963 Pontiac GTO.

overhead-cam shaft system 43 Way of opening engine valves that puts the opening parts right over the valves. Eliminates the use of long pushrods running down into the engine.

solid rear axle 26   Way of mounting rear wheels on a single beam. It has a low production cost, but it can cause both wheels to bounce when one hits a bump.

Wankel rotary engine 37   Engine type that replaces usual pistons and valves with a rotating triangular piston. Combines small size, lightness and power. GM considered using the rotary, but only Mazda now produces it.